Pebble®
Bilingüe/ Plus
Bilingual

Patrones en la naturaleza/Patterns in Nature

Las fases de la Luna/ Phases of the Moon

por/by Gillia M. Olson

Traducción/Translation: Dr. Martín Luis Guzmán Ferrer
Editor Consultor/Consulting Editor: Dra. Gail Saunders-Smith

Consultor en contenidos/Content Consultant:
Dr. Ronald Browne, Associate Professor of Elementary Education
Minnesota State University, Mankato, Minnesota

Capstone
press®

Mankato, Minnesota

Pebble Plus is published by Capstone Press,
151 Good Counsel Drive, P.O. Box 669, Mankato, Minnesota 56002.
www.capstonepress.com

1 2 3 4 5 6 13 12 11 10 09 08

Library of Congress Cataloging-in-Publication Data
Olson, Gillia M.
  [Phases of the moon. Spanish & English]
  Las fases de la luna = Phases of the moon / por Gillia M. Olson.
  p. cm. — (Pebble Plus. Patrones en la naturaleza = Pebble Plus. Patterns in nature)
  Includes index.
  ISBN-13: 978-1-4296-2372-8 (hardcover)
  ISBN-10: 1-4296-2372-1 (hardcover)
  1. Moon — Phases — Juvenile literature. 2. Pattern perception — Juvenile literature. I. Title. II. Title:
Phases of the moon. III. Series.
  QB588.O4718 2009
  523.3'2 — dc22   2008001217

Summary: Simple text and photographs introduce moon phases, including why they occur and what they
  are called — in both English and Spanish.

Editorial Credits
Heather Adamson, editor; Katy Kudela, bilingual editor; Eida del Risco, Spanish copy editor; Kia Adams,
  designer; Renée Doyle, illustrator; Jo Miller, photo researcher; Scott Thoms, photo editor

Photo Credits
Corbis/Richard Cummins, 10–11; Mike Zens, 12–13; zefa/Frans Lemmens, cover (full moon with city)
Index Stock Imagery/Ken Wardius, 14–15
Nature Places Library/Artur Tabor, 16–17, 18–19
Peter Arnold/Werner H. Muller, 5
Photodisc, cover (moon)
Photo Researchers Inc./Gerard Lodriguss, 8–9
Shutterstock/Vladimir Ivanov, backcover; Taipan Kid, 21 (all); Wayne James, 1
Unicorn Stock photos/Ed Harp, cover (moon with trees)

Note to Parents and Teachers

The Patrones en la naturaleza/Patterns in Nature set supports national science standards related to earth and life science. This book describes and illustrates moon phases in both English and Spanish. The images support early readers in understanding the text. The repetition of words and phrases helps early readers learn new words. This book also introduces early readers to subject-specific vocabulary words, which are defined in the Glossary section. Early readers may need assistance to read some words and to use the Table of Contents, Glossary, Internet Sites, and Index sections of the book.

Table of Contents

Tabla de contenidos

The Moon's Shape

The moon seems to

change shape. It doesn't.

The change is how much

of the moon you can see.

La forma de la Luna

La Luna parece que cambia

de forma. No es así.

El cambio es lo que tú

puedes ver de la Luna.

The sun lights up one side
of the moon. The moon circles
the Earth. Your view of the moon
changes. From Earth, you see
different moon phases.

El Sol ilumina un lado de la Luna.
La Luna le da la vuelta a la Tierra.
Por eso la vista de la Luna cambia.
Desde la Tierra, tú ves las diferentes
fases de la Luna.

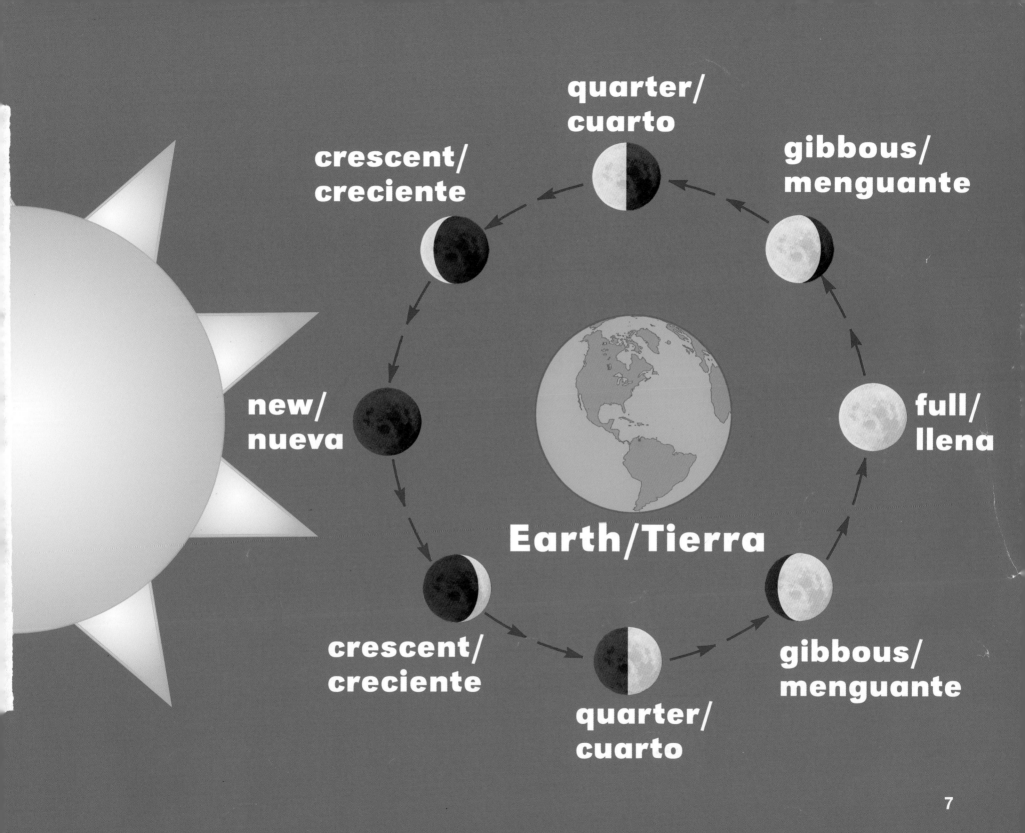

quarter/
cuarto

crescent/
creciente

gibbous/
menguante

new/
nueva

full/
llena

Earth/Tierra

crescent/
creciente

gibbous/
menguante

quarter/
cuarto

7

Moon Phases

The moon phases start with the new moon. The new moon looks all dark. A few days later a small sliver of moon appears.

Las fases de la Luna

Las fases de la Luna empiezan con la luna nueva. La luna nueva se ve toda oscura. Unos días después aparece un filito de la Luna.

The next phase looks like
a banana. It's called
a crescent moon.

La siguiente fase parece
un plátano. Se llama
luna creciente.

Then the moon looks
like half of a circle.
This phase is a
quarter moon.

Luego la Luna parece
la mitad de un círculo.
Esta fase se llama
un cuarto de luna.

13

The next phase is

a gibbous moon.

It looks like a circle

with a crescent cut out.

La siguiente fase es la luna

menguante. Se ve como

un círculo al que le han

cortado un pedazo.

15

Next, you see all
of the sunlit side.
It is a full moon.

Después tú puedes ver todo
el lado de la Luna iluminado
por el Sol. Es la luna llena.

It's a Pattern

After a full moon, you see

less and less of the sunlit

side. Then, there is a

new moon again.

Se forma un patrón

Después de la luna llena,

empiezas a ver menos y menos

del lado iluminado. Entonces,

vuelve a haber una luna nueva.

One after another, all the
moon phases repeat each
month. The phases are
one of nature's patterns.

Una tras otra, las fases de
la Luna se repiten cada mes.
Las fases son uno de los
patrones de la naturaleza.

Glossary

Earth — the planet where we live; the moon is about 239,000 miles (385,000 kilometers) from Earth.

nature — everything in the world that isn't made by people

pattern — something that happens again and again in the same order

phase — a stage; the moon's phases are the shapes that it appears to take over a month.

sun — a star that gives the moon and earth light and warmth; a star is a large ball of burning gases in space.

view — what you can see from a certain place; views change when you move and when objects, like the moon, move.

Glosario

la fase — etapa; las fases de la Luna son las formas que ésta parece adoptar durante un mes.

la naturaleza — todas las cosas del mundo que no han sido hechas por el hombre

el patrón — algo que se repite una y otra vez en el mismo orden

el Sol — estrella que da a la Luna y la Tierra luz y calor; una estrella es una bola enorme de gases que arden en el espacio.

la Tierra — planeta donde vivimos; la Luna está como a 385,000 kilómetros (239,000 millas) de la Tierra.

la vista — algo que puedes ver desde un lugar; las vistas cambian cuando te mueves y cuando los objetos, como la Luna, se mueven.

Internet Sites

FactHound offers a safe, fun way to find Internet sites related to this book. All of the sites on FactHound have been researched by our staff.

Here's how:

1. Visit *www.facthound.com*

2. Choose your grade level.

3. Type in this book ID **1429623721** for age-appropriate sites. You may also browse subjects by clicking on letters, or by clicking on pictures and words.

4. Click on the **Fetch It** button.

FactHound will fetch the best sites for you!

Index

Sitios de Internet

FactHound te brinda una manera divertida y segura de encontrar sitios de Internet relacionados con este libro. Hemos investigado todos los sitios de FactHound. Es posible que algunos sitios no estén en español.

Se hace así:

1. Visita *www.facthound.com*

2. Elige tu grado escolar.

3. Introduce este código especial **1429623721** para ver sitios apropiados a tu edad, o usa una palabra relacionada con este libro para hacer una búsqueda general.

4. Haz un clic en el botón **Fetch It**.

¡FactHound buscará los mejores sitios para ti!

Índice